THE BIG BOOK OF IRAN

AN EDUCATIONAL COUNTRY TRAVEL PICTURE BOOK FOR KIDS ABOUT HISTORY, DESTINATION PLACES, ANIMALS AND MANY MORE

Copyright @2023 James K. Mahi

All rights reserved

Iran is located in the Middle East and has a rich history that goes back thousands of years.

What is the national animal of the Iran?

There is no official national animal of Iran, but the Asiatic lion, Asiatic cheetah, Persian leopard, Persian cat, and Persian fallow deer are all considered national symbols.

What is the national bird of the Iran?

The national bird of Iran is the Hoopoe (Hoopoe is also the national bird of Israel).

What is the national sport of the Iran?

The national sport of Iran is wrestling.

What is the national tree of the Iran?

The national tree of Iran is the Cypress tree.

What is the official name of the Iran?

The official name of Iran is the Islamic Republic of Iran.

What are the people of the Iran called?

The people of Iran are called Iranians.

How big is the Iran?

Iran is the 18th largest country in the world, with a total area of 1,648,195 square kilometers.

Which city is the largest in the Iran?

The largest city in Iran is Tehran, the capital.

What is the population of Iran?

The population of Iran is 83,992,949 (2023 est.).

Is the Iran overly populated?

Yes, Iran is considered to be an overpopulated country, with a population density of 49.5 people per square kilometer.

How many provinces does the Iran have?

Iran has 31 provinces.

What percentage of the Iran is covered by rainforests?

Only 0.1% of Iran is covered by rainforests.

What percentage of the world's land does the Iran occupy?

Iran occupies about 0.5% of the world's land.

How many time zones are there in the Iran?

1 time zones in Iran

What is Iran's nickname?

Iran's nickname is "The Land of Kings".

Who ruled Iran first?

The first rulers of Iran were the Medes, who were followed by the Achaemenids, the Parthians, and the Sassanids.

What is the oldest city in Iran?

The oldest city in Iran is Susa, which was founded in the 4th millennium BC.

What is the highest temperature ever recorded in the Iran?

The highest temperature ever recorded in Iran was 54 degrees Celsius (129 degrees Fahrenheit), which was recorded in Ahvaz in 1974.

What is the lowest temperature ever recorded in the Iran?

The lowest temperature ever recorded in Iran was -27 degrees Celsius (-17 degrees Fahrenheit), which was recorded in Meshginshahr in 1978.

Which months are the coldest in the Iran?

The coldest months in Iran are December, January, and February.

Which months are the hottest in the Iran?

The hottest months in Iran are July and August.

What was the old name of the Iran?

The old name of Iran was Persia.

The capital city of Iran is Tehran, and it's a bustling place with lots to see and do.

Iran is known for its beautiful carpets, which are often made by hand and are very intricate.

The official language spoken in Iran is Persian, also known as Farsi.

Iran is famous for its historic city of Persepolis, which was the capital of the ancient Persian Empire.

The country is home to a variety of delicious foods, such as kebabs, rice dishes, and stews.

Iran has both hot deserts and snowy mountains, making its landscapes diverse and stunning.

Iranians celebrate the New Year, called "Nowruz," on the first day of spring.

Iran is known for its beautiful mosques with intricate designs and stunning architecture.

The ancient city of Isfahan in Iran is famous for its stunning bridges and historical buildings.

Iran has a rich tradition of poetry, with famous poets like Rumi and Hafez.

The Caspian Sea, one of the largest lakes in the world, borders Iran to the north.

Iranian tea is a popular drink, often enjoyed with sweets like baklava.

The Tower of Silence near Yazd is a unique historical site where Zoroastrians practiced their burial rituals.

Iran has one of the world's oldest civilizations, dating back to the Elamite kingdom around 2700 BC.

The country is home to many ancient ruins and historical sites that tell stories of its past.

Iran is famous for its beautiful gardens, like the Eram Garden in Shiraz.

Persian rugs are highly prized and are considered works of art all around the world.

Iran's Grand Bazaar in Tehran is one of the oldest and largest bazaars in the world.

Traditional music and dance are important parts of Iranian culture and celebrations.

The country is known for producing high-quality saffron, which is used as a spice and for coloring.

The Golestan Palace in Tehran is a UNESCO World Heritage site known for its stunning architecture.

Iranians celebrate the Festival of Fire, called "Chaharshanbe Suri," by jumping over bonfires.

The city of Yazd is famous for its unique windcatcher architecture that helps cool buildings.

Iran has 24 UNESCO World Heritage sites, showcasing its rich history and culture.

The Iranian currency is called the Iranian Rial (IRR).

The ancient Persian Empire, led by kings like Cyrus the Great, was once one of the largest in the world.

Iran's deserts have special formations called kaluts, which are large sandy shapes created by wind and water.

Iran is known for its warm hospitality, and visitors often experience the kindness of the people.

The Iran has a large nomadic population with unique traditions and lifestyles.

The colorful Nasir ol Molk Mosque in Shiraz is sometimes called the "Rainbow Mosque."

Iran's New Year celebrations can last for around 13 days, filled with joy, family, and special customs.

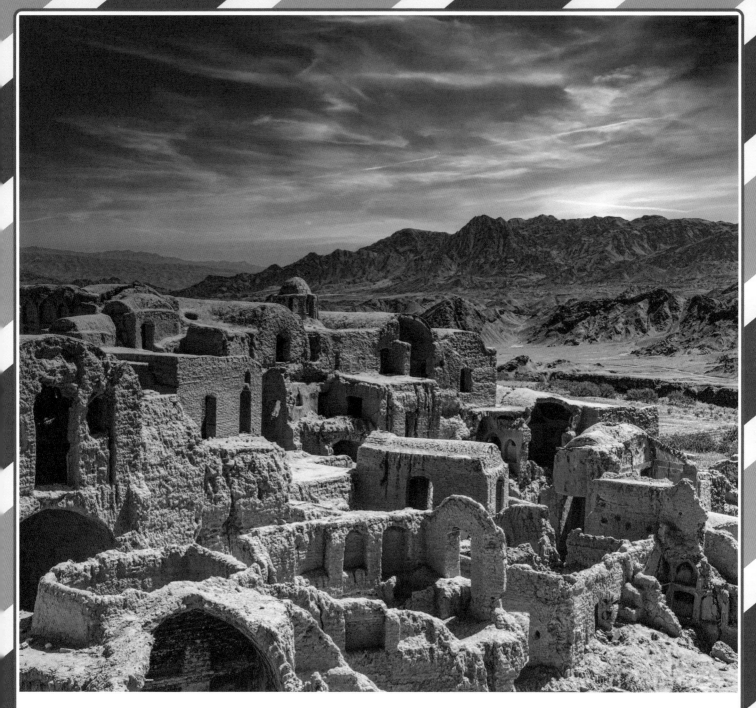

The ancient city of Bam had a famous mud-brick citadel that unfortunately was destroyed by an earthquake.

Iranians enjoy traditional sports like wrestling and "Varzesh-e Bastani," a type of physical training.

The Tabiat Bridge in Tehran is a modern architectural marvel and a popular gathering spot.

Iran's rich history is tied to the Silk Road, an ancient trading route connecting East and West.

The city of Kerman is known for its historical bathhouses, some of which are still in use today.

- The Shah Mosque in Isfahan is renowned for its stunning blue tiles and intricate calligraphy.
- Iran is home to diverse ethnic groups, each with its own traditions, languages, and customs.
- The ancient city of Susa was mentioned in the Bible and is known for its archaeological discoveries.
- Iranians celebrate "Sizdah Be-dar," a day to spend outdoors on the 13th day of the New Year festivities.
- The city of Qom is an important religious center and a destination for pilgrims.
- Iran's nature includes the Alborz and Zagros mountain ranges, perfect for hiking and exploring.
- The traditional bazaars in cities like Tabriz offer a glimpse into daily life and local products.
- Iranian art often features intricate patterns, floral motifs, and geometric designs.
- The ancient city of Hamedan is believed to be one of the oldest in Iran, with a rich history.
- The Persian Gulf, with its warm waters and beautiful beaches, is a popular vacation spot.
- Iranians have a strong love for poetry, and their poets are respected and celebrated in their culture.

TOP 15 TRAVEL TIPS FOR VISITING IRAN:

1. **Visa Preparation:** Get your visa in advance. Check if you need one before you travel.
2. **Dress Modestly:** Wear modest clothing to respect local customs, especially for women – cover your hair and wear loose-fitting clothes.
3. **Local Etiquette:** Be respectful of local customs and traditions. Greet people with a smile and politeness.
4. **Currency Exchange:** Exchange some local currency (Iranian Rial) upon arrival for small expenses.
5. **Language:** Learn a few basic Persian phrases. It can help you connect with locals.
6. **Food and Water:** Try local dishes, but also be cautious with street food. Drink bottled water to stay safe.
7. **Transportation:** Use taxis and ridesharing apps for convenience. Negotiate taxi fares before you start the ride.
8. **Cultural Sites:** Respect religious sites, and ask for permission before taking photos of people.
9. **Bargaining:** Bargaining is common in markets, so don't hesitate to negotiate prices.
10. **Internet Access:** Get a local SIM card for internet access. Some international websites might be blocked.
11. **Safety:** Iran is generally safe, but stay aware of your surroundings, especially in crowded places.
12. **Health Precautions:** Check if any vaccinations are needed before your trip and carry necessary medications.
13. **Photography Rules:** Respect photography rules, especially near government buildings and military sites.
14. **Electricity:** The standard voltage is 220V. Bring a universal adapter for your electronics.
15. **Local Laws:** Be aware of local laws, such as alcohol consumption and public behavior.

Printed in Great Britain
by Amazon

39546303R00025